Traditional Honey R

Frances Brown

BBNO
The Weaven
Little Dewchurch
Hereford
HR2 6PP

©Frances Brown

ISBN 978-0-905652-70-2

Contents

Foreword

For breakfast in Scotland, a meal like no other, Scott's *Fair Maid of Perth* served "thin soft cakes made of flour and honey", a recipe which has not survived. However, Frances Brown's book gives recipes for Porridge Oat Biscuits, Selkirk Bannock and other delights.

Those of you lucky enough to visit the Open Arms at Dirleton in the 1960s will not forget their Cranachan. This appears here and tastes just as delightful with some Tayside raspberries to add on top.

There are some words that may not have reached south of the border. For example a "Clauti" or "Clootie" is a coarse oat meal made in Kinross. A "Bannock" is an oatcake or a pancake, but it is more than that. A "Beltane Bannock" was baked for the first day of summer, a "Lammas Bannock" baked for the first day of autumn and children used to be given "Teething Bannocks" with holes in them to bite until broken when they were teething.

Burns used to speak of "Crowdie-time" meaning breakfast time and in the HIghlands they made crowdie cheese. Was it this that Kate carried up the gate to a wounded brother at the Battle of Sheriffmuir?:-

> "My sister Kate cam up the gate
> Wi' crowdie unto me man
> She swore she saw the rebels ran
> Frae Perth unto Dundee man."

John Kinross

Honey is a natural sweetener used since prehistoric times. It is something we should prize also, considering a honeybee can travel many miles for the teaspoonful of honey it will gather in its tifetime.

Most recipes make use of mild honey but some benefit from the stronger Scottish Heather Honey.

Acknowledgements

John Kinross has persuaded me to write this book which I could not have managed without the help of my daughter, Enid, Advertising and Publicity Convener for The Scottish Beekeepers' Association, who has typed out all these recipes on her computer during a honey flow.

I thank also my grand daughter, Alexandra, for her pencil drawings and for friends who have given recipes or tested them. To Puddledub Pork of Fife for their delicious gammon and to Christopher Trotter, Chef at Myres Castle, Fife who entertained Fife Beekeepers at Scotland's Larder with cookery demonstrations and allowed me to use the recipes he tried out.

Frances Brown
Kirkcaldy,
Fife 2004

KING SCALLOPS WITH LEEK, GINGER AND HONEY

Per person

4 Scallops
1/2 leek cut into fine strips
2 slices of ginger cut into fine strips
Olive oil
Teaspoon of Honey
Dash of Soy Sauce

Method
Gently cook the scallops in olive oil on both sides. Remove them then add the leek and stir till lightly brown and allow to go limp. Add the ginger and season. Add the honey and soy sauce. Slice the scallops and return to the pan, mix gently through to reheat.

SCOTTISH SMOKED SALMON WITH BEETROOT LIME RELISH

Serves 4

370 gms (3/4 lb) slices smoked salmon
1 – 2 tbs of runny honey
1 tbs of finely chopped dill
1 lime grated and juiced
255 gms (8 oz) cooked beetroot
1/2 peeled cucumber
Salt and pepper
Rocket

Method
Mix together the honey, lime juice and zest. Strip and peel the beetroot and cut into fine matchsticks. Slice the cucumber into rounds then into matchsticks. Slice the smoked salmon into strips. Gently combine all the ingredients with the dressing and season with salt and pepper. Serve on a bed of rocket.

CRABBIE'S GREEN GINGER AND HONEY CHICKEN

Serves 4

4 chicken breasts
1 cup of Crabbie's Green Ginger wine
1 dsp of honey
Small tub single cream

Method
In a heavy based frying pan on a medium heat cook the chicken breasts in the Crabbie's ginger wine and honey, turning occasionally. When cooked turn up the heat to caramelize the liquid. Add the cream and stir till blended. Serve on a bed of rice or green salad.

WALNUT CHICKEN

Serves 4

60 gm (2oz) broken walnuts
Small slices onion
1 small sliced red pepper
4 tbsp corn oil
360 gm (3/4 lb) cooked chicken cut into strips
1/2 pint chicken stock
1 dsp corn flour
1 tsp honey
1 tbs soy sauce
2 tbs sherry
Method
Fry walnuts, onion and pepper till tender but not brown. Stir in the chicken, add the stock. Mix cornflour, honey and soy sauce and add to the rest. Simmer for three minutes. Add sherry. Serve on a bed of rice.

HONEY AND CHICKEN CHILLI

Serves 4

Pieces of chicken either on or off the bone
1 egg white
1 tbs corn flour
2 cloves of garlic crushed
2 tbs of runny honey
2 tbs of wine vinegar
2 tbs of soy sauce
4 tbs of vegetable oil
120 gm (4 oz) walnuts
4 small dried red chilli
4 spring onions finely chopped
Chopped parsley

Method
Beat the egg white with the corn flour and mix into the chicken with half of the garlic. Cover and set aside.
Combine the honey with the vinegar and soy sauce. Heat a large frying pan. Add 3 tbs of oil and cook the chicken in batches removing it as soon as it colours. Wipe the pan clean and add the rest of the oil and allow it to get very hot. Stir the walnuts briefly to take a little colour and remove. Add the chilli, garlic and spring onion. Return all the other items to the pan, finally adding the honey, soy sauce mix. Bring it to the boil and reduce the sauce a little. Serve with rice.

HONEY BAKED CHICKEN

Serves 4

8 Chicken pieces
1 packet of Continental French onion soup and reconstitute
3 tbs of honey
3/4 cup white wine

Method (Microwave)
Mix onion soup, honey and white wine and pour evenly over the chicken in a shallow, oven proof dish. Microwave on high for 10 minutes, then medium wave for 20 minutes.

Method (Oven)
Put the chicken with 1 pint of water in a casserole dish in oven, gas 4, 170-180°C, for 1/2 hour. Remove chicken. Mix the water with soup powder with honey and wine. Replace the chicken and cook for a further 1 hour.

CHRISTMAS SALAD WITH HONEY DRESSING

Mixed leaves
Half red onion
2 tsp pine nuts
90 gms (3 oz) St. Andrews cheese
Red cabbage
Half a leek
Quails eggs (at least two per person)

Method
Finely chop the red onion. Cut the leek into fine strips and blanche. Dice the cheese. Shred the cabbage finely. Poach the quails eggs and refresh. Use honey dressing and combine ingredients.

HONEY DRESSING

1 tbs wine vinegar
3 tbs olive oil
1 tsp mustard powder
Pinch of salt and pepper
1 dsp honey

Method
Blend all ingredients together.

SCOTCH WHISKY, BLACK PEPPER AND HONEY DRESSING

120 gm (4 oz) mayonnaise
30 gm (1 oz) grainy mustard
1 tsp ground black pepper
1 tbs Scotch whisky
1 tbs clear honey
1 tbs chopped parsley

Method
Blend all together and serve with cold Scottish Roast Beef.

CRABBIE'S HEATHER HONEY GLAZED HAM FROM 'PUDDLEDUB PORK'

Preparation time 8 – 10 hours soaking. Cooking time 25 mins per 1/2 kilo plus 25 mins.

1 ham boned and rolled
1/4 pint Crabbie's Green Ginger
120 gm (4 oz) heather honey
30 gm (1 oz) hazelnut oil
60 gm (2 oz) dark Muscavado sugar
1 tsp mustard

Method
Soak the ham, changing the water occasionally. Drain and allow to dry and put in roasting tin. Mix all the other ingredients. Brush 1/2 this mixture over ham and cover with foil and place in a preheated oven at 190°C.
Cooking time per weight of ham. After 1/3 of the cooking time brush the remaining glaze over the ham. After 2/3 of the time baste well and open the foil. Remove and allow to rest for 10 -15 mins. before carving.

PUDDLEDUB GAMMON

Cooking time 25 mins per 1/2 kilo plus 25 mins.

Soak in water overnight. In fresh water simmer gently for 3/4 of the cooking time. Remove from the water and place on foil in a roasting tin. Strip off the rind and spread over with honey then pat on dry mustard.
Cook at 180°C for the remainder of the time.

PUDDLEDUB PORK AND PRUNE CASSEROLE

Serves 6 – 8

2 tbs Sunflower oil
1 1/4 kilo (3 lb) shoulder pork, trimmed and cut into 3 cm cubes
60 gms (2 oz) plain flour
3/4 pint chicken stock
3 tbs white wine vinegar
3 tbs clear honey
2 tbs soy sauce
240 gm (8 oz) large mushrooms quartered
240 gm (8 oz) ready to eat stoned prunes
Salt and black pepper
Chopped parsley to garnish

Method
Heat the oil in a large flame proof casserole. Add the pork in batches and cook over medium to high heat for 5 mins or until golden brown all over. Return all the meat to the casserole, sprinkle in the flour and cook, stirring for 1 minute. Stir in the chicken stock, white wine vinegar, honey, soy sauce and salt and pepper to taste and bring to the boil. Cover and cook in a preheated oven at 160°C for 2 hours. Stir in the mushrooms and prunes and cook for a further hour or until the pork is tender. Taste for seasoning and garnish with parsley before serving.

MARINADE FOR PORK OR CHICKEN

1/4 pint olive oil
1/4 pint red wine
1 tbs tomato puree
1 tbs runny honey
1 tbs wholegrain mustard
1 tbs wine vinegar
clove of garlic crushed

Method
Mix all together and marinade pork or chicken for a few hours before grilling or roasting.

SCOTTISH LAMB LEG STEAK AND MARINADE

4 Scottish lamb leg steaks

Marinade :
2 tbs Olive oil
6 tbs orange juice
3 tbs clear honey
2 tbs red wine
1 clove of garlic crushed
1tbs of fresh chopped herbs

Method
Place marinade in a bowl and mix well. Place Scottish lamb leg steaks in a shallow dish and pour over the marinade. Leave overnight. Remove from the marinade and cook under a medium grill for 16 – 18 mins turning occasionally.

Soups, Sauces and Preserves

SOY AND HONEY KALE

A good quantity of kale
Butter
Soy sauce
1 tsp honey

Method
Make sure the kale is cut to slightly larger than bite size pieces, especially the stalks which should be thin. Wash and dry them. Put the oil in a large hot pan and add the butter. Quickly throw in the vegetable and stir to coat in the oil and cook. As it begins to soften add the soy and honey to coat. Serve quickly.

OATMEAL AND HONEY SOUP

1 medium onion
30 gm (1 oz) butter
2 chicken cubes
60 gm (2 oz) medium oatmeal
2 pints water
small carton of single cream
1 tbs honey
Chopped fresh dill
Salt and pepper

Method
Saute the sliced onion in butter till clear. Add the water, chicken cubes and oatmeal. Simmer for 30 mins. Remove from heat. Add honey, dill, cream, salt and pepper. Liquidise and serve with crusty bread.

APRICOT CHUTNEY

240 gm (1/2 lb) dried chopped apricots
120 gm (4 oz) seedless raisins
480 gm (1 lb) onions
120 gm (4 oz) honey
3/4 pint water
1/2 pint distilled malt vinegar
Freshly ground black pepper
1 teaspoon ground cummin

Method
Soak apricots in water overnight. Chop onions and put onion, raisins and apricots in a pan with honey, vinegar and rest of the water. Cook over a gentle heat until thick and pulpy. Add pepper and cummin. Pot and seal.

CARROT, GINGER AND ALMOND CHUTNEY

480 gms (1 lb) carrots grated
1 tsp ground coriander
1 tsp sea salt
Generous pinch of cayenne pepper
Finely grated zest and juice of 1 lemon
9 fl. oz cider vinegar
360 gm (12 oz) sugar
Generous tablespoon of clear honey
30 gms. (1 oz) flaked almonds
60 gm (2 oz) fresh ginger grated

Method
Put the carrots, coriander, salt, cayenne pepper, lemon zest, ginger, juice and vinegar into a non metalic bowl. Cover and leave in a cool place overnight.

Tip the contents of the bowl into a pan, add 5 fl oz water and bring to the boil and simmer for 20 minutes. Over a low heat stir in the sugar and honey until both have dissolved. Simmer for a further 20 – 25 minutes, stirring occasionally until the mixture is thick. Stir in the almonds and simmer for another 4 minutes.

Pot into warm jars, cover and leave to mature for a month.

TOMATO SAUCE

60 gm (2 oz) butter
1 onion peeled and chopped
2 garlic cloves crushed
1 tbs honey
2 x 14 oz cans chopped tomatoes
3 tablespoons tomato paste
2 oregano sprigs chopped
Salt and pepper

Method
Saute onion and garlic in butter until clear. Add remaining ingredients and cook for 25 – 30 mins until thick and pulpy. Suitable for freezing in small containers.

Delicious over Scottish Haddock and baked in the oven.

HONEY LEMON CURD

½ pint honey
Beaten yolks of 3 eggs
Whites of 2 eggs
Juice of 2 lemons
Rind of 1 lemon
50 gm (1½ oz) butter

Method
Heat in a bowl over a pan of boiling water till thick, stirring all the time. Pour into small warmed jars.

HONEY DUNDEE MARMALADE

480 gm (1 lb) Seville oranges
1 lemon
1 kg of sugar
360 gm (¾ lb) honey

Method
Weigh the pan. Cut oranges and lemon in half. Remove juice, pips and pith. Tie pips and pith in a piece of muslin. Chop or slice thinly the peel and soak overnight with the muslin bag in ¾ pint water. Simmer till the peel is soft. Remove the muslin bag, add the juice. Add a little water, if necessary, to make the contents 1 kg 350 gm. (3 lbs). Add the bag of sugar and honey and boil steadily till setting point is reached. Test by putting a little on a saucer. Allow to cool when it should wrinkle when pushed. Pour into warm jars and seal.

APPLE HONEY JELLY

2 kg apples
4 pints water
Sugar
Clear honey
Cloves
Ginger
Cinnamon stick

Method
Boil the apples in water until soft. Strain in a jelly bag overnight. To each pint of liquid add 110 gm (4 oz) of honey and 330 gm (12 oz) sugar plus cinnamon stick, 3 cloves and small piece of ginger tied in a muslin bag. Heat gently until sugar and honey dissolved then bring to the boil. Cook on a rolling boil for approx. 10 mins. or until setting point is reached. Remove from the heat. Remove any scum from the surface and ladle into warm, sterilised jars. Cover and seal.

CHOCOLATE SPREAD

120 gm (4 oz) margarine
2 tbs honey
1 heaped dsp cocoa

Method
Bring to the boil, pot and cool.

Drinks

WHISKY MAC

1 measure of Crabbie's Green Ginger
1 measure blended whisky
1 tsp honey

Method
Pour into a whisky tumbler, stir well and enjoy.

CUCUMBER AND HONEY DRINK

If you grow cucumbers in your greenhouse you may well have a prolific crop. A delicious drink can be made by liquidising the cucumber and adding honey and lemon to taste.

CLOOTIE DUMPLING

Have ready a pudding cloth scalded in boiling water, rung out and sprinkled with flour. Also a large pot half full of boiling water with a saucer in the bottom.

360 gm (12 oz) Self Raising Flour
180 gm (6 oz) vegetable suet
120 gm (4 oz) each currants, sultanas and stones raisins
1/2 apple grated
1 rounded tsp each cinnamon, ginger and spice
90 gm (3 oz) soft brown sugar
Rounded tbs honey
1/2 tsp each of baking soda and cream of tartar
1 egg beaten
3 tbs treacle
1/4 pint milk to mix to a soft dough

Method
Mix all together and turn out onto a floured cloth. Tie loosely and plunge into pot of boiling water and boil steadily for 3 hours. Lift carefully out and untie. Turn out onto a hot dish. Remove cloth and dry off in moderate oven for 10 mins.

CRANACHAN

1 pt double cream
3 oz pinhead or medium oatmeal
6 tbs whisky
3 tbs heather honey
1 lb raspberries

Method
Toast oatmeal under grill and cool. Whisk together cream, whisky and honey. Fold in cooled oatmeal and 3/4 raspberries. Spoon into round wine glasses or individual dishes and decorate with the remaining raspberries.

SCOTTISH BRAMBLE MOUSSE

480 gm (1 lb) brambles
1 – 2 tbs honey
2 eggs
180 gm (6 oz) double cream
1 packet (1/2 oz) gelatine

Method
Put brambles with honey into a saucepan and heat gently till the juice runs from them and they are soft enough to pass through a fine sieve. Dissolve the gelatine in a little water. Separate the yolks and whites of eggs. Beat the yolks and add to the bramble puree stirring until the puree thickens until like custard. Add gelatine, stirring well. Whip cream until thick and stir into the puree. Beat the egg whites till stiff and fold in. Pour into a mould and leave to set.

HONEY AND PRALINE MOUSSE

PRALINE
60 gms (2 oz) whole almonds, unblanched
60 gms (2oz) caster sugar

Method
Put almonds and sugar into a small pan over a moderate until the sugar is completely melted. Continue, stirring a little, until it is golden brown. Pour out onto a well oiled baking sheet spreading out the almonds. When cool remove and put in a bowl. Break up with the end of the rolling pin. Tip out onto a flat surface and crush with the rolling pin. This will keep in a screw topped jar.

MOUSSE
8 fl oz milk
Vanilla pod or concentrate
3 leaves of gelatine or 1/2 oz packet
4 egg yolks
2 tbs honey
1/2 pint double cream
1/2 Praline

Method
Bring to simmering point the milk and add the vanilla. Beat the egg yolks with the honey till pale. Soak the gelatine leaves in cold water or sprinkle the gelatine packet on warm water to dissolve. Add the warmed milk to the beaten egg and honey. Stir well. Add the softened gelatine leaves or the dissolved gelatine making sure it is all dissolved. Allow to cool and add the praline and sofly whipped cream. Pour into serving glasses and top with a sprinkle of praline.

RASPBERRY SPECIAL

120 gm (1/4 lb) raspberries
2 tbs honey
A few dsp cream or evaporated milk

Method
Crush the berries in a bowl to free the juice. In a saucepan put 2 tbs honey and 1/4 pint water and allow to boil for 5 minutes. When cool add the syrup to the fruit and cream mixture. Whisk well and pour into a freezing tray. Freeze until required.

GOOSEBERRY FOOL

480 gm (1 lb) gooseberries
Honey
Thick cream

Method
Cook gooseberries in a little water until soft. Press through a fine sieve and sweeten to taste with honey. Mix with an equal quantity of thick cream. Serve in glasses.

May also be made with raspberries, tayberries, brambles, blackcurrants or apple.

SCOTTISH TRIFLE

2 honey sponge cakes (see separate recipe)
Some raspberry jam
Glass of sherry
Scottish raspberries
Fruit juice
1/2 - 3/4 pint custard, not too thick
Whipped cream

Method
Slice the sponges through the middle and spread with raspberry jam. Put a layer in the bottom of a glass trifle dish and soak with a glass of sherry. Layer sponges with Scottish rasperries till dish is nearly full. Soak with fruit juice. Cover with 1/2 - 3/4 pint custard, not too thick. When cool pipe whipped cream on top and decorate with raspberries.

LEMON FLAN

240 gm (8 oz) shortcrust pastry
2 eggs
60 gm (2 oz) honey
60 gm (2 oz) caster sugar
60 gm (2 oz) melted butter
Juice of a large lemon

Method
Make the pastry and roll out to line a 1 pint pie plate. Bake blind at 370°F or 170°C for 15 – 20 minutes. Make the filling by whisking eggs, sugar and honey till thick and creamy. Add lemon juice and melted butter and whisk again to mix. Pour carefully into pastry case and bake at 335°F or 160°C for 20 – 30 minutes till set. Serve cold.

LEMON LOVELY

60 gm (2 oz) margarine
120 gm (4 oz) thin honey
60 gm (2 oz) Self Raising Flour
2 eggs separated
Rind and juice of 1 lemon
Cup of milk

Method
Cream margarine and honey. Add the flour and the 2 yolks. Stir in the grated rind and juice of 1 lemon and a cup of milk. Beat whites of eggs stiffly and fold in. Pour into a greased casserole dish, bake in a moderate oven 325°F or 160°C for 40 minutes.

HONEY RASPBERRY MERINGUE ICECREAM

480 gm (1 lb) raspberries
1/2 pint double cream
1/2 dozen meringues
Honey

Method
Puree raspberries, sieve and sweeten with honey. Lightly whip double cream. Break meringue into bits, not too small. Fold altogether and pour into container and freeze.

SIMPLE HONEY ICECREAM

1 large tin of Carnation milk
1 1/2 tbs caster sugar
1 1/2 tbs Scottish liquid honey

Method
Chill a large tin or Carnation milk then whisk it in a chilled bowl with a chilled whisk until the amount has doubled. Add sugar and honey and whisk again until thick. Cover the bowl and put in the freezer until ready to eat when frozen.

HONEY PEARS IN SPICED RED WINE

6 large firm pears
Juice of 1/2 lemon
60 gm (2 oz) honey
500 ml (18 fl oz) red wine
Thinly pared strip of lemon zest
2 cinnamon sticks
2 tsp arrowroot

Method
Peel the pears thinly and cut a thin slice off the base so they stand upright. Brush with the lemon juice. Place the honey and wine in a large pan. Heat gently to dissolve then add the pears, lemon zest and cinnamon sticks. Bring to the boil and reduce the heat. Cover with a lid and gently poach for 1 hour till tender, turning occasionally. Lift out carefully and set upright on a serving dish. Boil the remaining liquid to about 1/2 pint. Blend the remaining lemon juice with the arrowroot and whisk into the liquid into the pan until it boils and thickens. Spoon over the pears and serve hot or cold.

TWICE BAKED HONEY CHOCOLATE SOUFFLE

SOUFFLE
60 gm (2 oz) good plain chocolate
225 ml (8 fl oz) milk
4 tbs caster sugar
60 gm (2 oz) butter
4 tbs plain flour
4 eggs separated
1 tbs cocoa powder

SAUCE
1/2 pint double cream
1 tbs cocoa powder whisked to a paste with a little water
60 (2 oz) plain chocolate (as in the souffle)
2 tbs of honey
Prepare 6 to 8 ramekins lined with clingfilm

Method
For the souffle melt the chocolate. Heat the milk to just before boiling and add the chocolate. Set aside. Melt the butter in a small pan and add the flour, add the milk and stir to create a smooth shiny mixture. Place in a bowl and allow to cool a little. Add the yolks and mix in with a spatula. Whisk the whites in a glass bowl and when peaked whisk in the sugar briefly then fold in the cocoa powder. Beat a third of the white mix into the chocolate mix and fold the rest in. Pour carefully into the ramekins and bake at gas 6, 375°F or 190°C for 15 – 20 minutes or until lightly browned and risen.

For the sauce put the cream in a pan with the honey and chocolate, stir to combine. Lastly whisk in the cocoa paste and simmer gently. When the souffles are ready turn into an ovenproof dish and pour over the sauce. Bake in the same oven until risen and bubbling.

Cakes Bread and Biscuits

WHOLEWHEAT HONEY SPONGES

120 gm (4 oz) brown flour
2 1/2 tsp baking powder
2 eggs
120 gms (4 oz) soft brown sugar
120 gms (4 oz) softened butter

Method
Take 4 ramekins and butter them and put a teaspoon of honey in each one. Put all the other ingredients in a bowl and beat until well mixed. Spoon onto the honey and cover with buttered foil. Steam in the oven for about 1 hour. Serve with hot custard.

SCOTCH PORRIDGE OAT BISCUITS

360 gm (12 oz) porridge oats
120 gm (4 oz) plain flour
270 gm (9 oz) packet of Stork or a firm baking margarine
90 gm (3 oz) of soft set honey
60 gm (2 oz) sugar

Method
Mix all together. Roll out to 1/4 inch thickness on a well floured board. Cut into rounds. Bake at 325°F or 160°C for 15 – 20 minutes till golden.

FLAPJACK

7 inch square tin

150 gm (5 oz) margarine
60 gm (2 oz) soft brown sugar
2 tbs honey
150 gm (5 oz) SR Flour
150 gm (5 oz) rolled oats
Large tsp ground ginger
A few broken walnuts
Any of the following eg. Chopped ginger, cherries, raisins, pine kernels, sunflower seeds.

Method
Melt margarine, sugar and honey in a large pan – do not boil. Add rest of the ingredients. Spread out in the tin. Bake at 340°F or 170°C for 20 – 25 minutes. Leave in the tin until almost cool and mark into squares.

HONEY BRANDY SNAPS

Required:- Either wooden spoon handles or 1/2 - 3/4 wooden doweling cut into 6 x 6 inch lengths, sandpapered and slightly tapered at one end. Rub these with a buttery paper. 3 greased baking sheets.

120 gm (4 oz) caster sugar
120 gm (4 oz) butter
120 gm (4 oz) honey
120 gm (4 oz) SR Flour
1 tsp ginger

Method
Rub the butter into the flour and ginger. Mix in the sugar and honey. Make into a roll about 12 inches long *very lightly floured.* It helps to put this in the fridge for 1 hour to make it easier to handle.

Cut off 1 inch pieces, half these and roll into balls. Place a maximum of 6 on each tray and flatten. They spread out. Bake at 375°F 190°C for about 12 minutes or until golden. Remove from the oven, cool very slightly. Lift up the edge onto the dowel and roll up. Place onto a wire tray to set. If they become too brittle to handle put in the oven again for a short time. Fill with whipped cream and enjoy.

ABERNETHY BISCUITS

240 gm (8 oz) SR Flour
90 gm (3 oz) butter
30gm (1 oz) caster sugar
1 tbs runny honey
1 level tsp caraway seeds
1 egg beaten with a tablespoon milk

Method
Rub the butter into the flour, add the other ingredients to form a stiff dough. Roll out thinly. Cut out with 3 inch pastry cutter. Bake about 10 minutes at 350°F or 180°C.

SCOTTISH OATCAKES

240 gm (1/2 lb) medium or fine oatmeal
120 gm (1/4 lb) plain flour
1/2 tsp salt
1/2 tsp baking soda
1 tsp honey
90 gm (3 oz) margarine
hot water to mix

Method
Melt the margarine and honey in a little hot water and add to the dry ingredients. Add enough extra hot water to make a firm dough but do not make moist. Roll out 1/4 inch thick and cut out with a plain cutter, 2" – 3", or use a pot lid to make the circle and quarter. Bake in a moderate oven at 325°F or 160°C till dried out.

CHOCOLATE SHORTBREAD

240 gm (1/2 lb) butter (or half butter and half marg)
270 gm (9 oz) plain flour
90 gm (3 oz) cornflour
60 (2 oz) caster sugar
1 dsp honey
1/2 packet chocolate chips (add later)

Method
Blend all together till soft. Mix in chocolate chips. Roll out 1/4 inch thick and cut out with a biscuit cutter. Bake at 325°F or 160°C for 15 – 20 minutes.

PAVING STONES

240 gm (8 oz) Self Raising Flour
1 tsp mixed spice
90 gm (3 oz) brown sugar
90 gm (3 oz) margarine
1 dsp honey
1 tsp baking powder
A little milk to make a firm dough

Method
Blend all together adding a little milk if necessary. Roll into balls (about 12). Roll out into an oval shape about 1/4 inch thick. Put onto a greased baking sheet and bake at 325°F or 160°C for 10 – 15 mins. Ice when cold.

FAIR ISLE PEAT

120 gm (4 oz) margarine
240 gm (8 oz) digestive biscuits
1 tbs honey
1 tbs cocoa
1 tbs sugar
Sultanas, cherries or nuts if wished
120 gm (4 oz) chocolate for topping

Method
Melt margarine and mix in sugar, cocoa, honey and dried fruit, if used. Crush biscuits and add. Mix well and press into a 7" square tin. Melt chocolate and spread over. When cool cut into pieces.

GINGER NUTS

240 gm (8oz) Self Raising Flour
Pinch of salt
2 level tsp ginger
1 level tsp baking soda
120 gm (4 oz) caster sugar
1 standard egg
2 level tsp honey
2 level tsp treacle
90 gm (3 oz) margarine

Method
Measure treacle, honey and margarine into pan. Melt and remove from heat and cool a little. Stir in sieved flour, salt, ginger, baking soda and sugar. Add egg. Mix well and roll into balls. Put onto a greased baking sheet leaving space for spreading. Bake at 325°F or 160°C for 15 to 20 minutes.

HONEY SPONGE CAKES

Prepare 2 x 6" sandwich tins lined with silicone paper. Heat oven to 350°F or180°C.

3 large eggs
90 gm (3 oz) caster sugar
30 gm (1 oz) honey
120 gm (4 oz) plain flour sived with 1/2 tsp baking powder

Method
Whisk sugar, eggs and honey thoroughly over pan of hot water until thick and creamy. Fold in sieved flour, a little at a time, using a metal spoon. Pour into the two tins. Bake for 15 minutes.

HONEY CARROT CAKE

1 deep loaf tin required.

240 gm (8 oz) wheaten flour
240gm (8 oz) carrot grated
4 tsp mixed spice
4 tsp baking powder
120 gm (4 oz) margarine
120 gm (4 oz) brown sugar
120 gm (4 oz) honey
Optional extra – sultanas

Method

Melt margarine, sugar and honey and add to the dry ingredients. Place in loaf tin and bake at 325°F or 160°C for 1 hour.

HONEY AND LEMON LOAF

1 loaf tin, 9" x 4", required

120 gm (4 oz) margarine
60 gm (2 oz) caster sugar
Grated rind of a lemon
2 level tbs clear honey
2 eggs
150 gm (5 oz) Self Raising Flour

Topping
Juice of 1 lemon
2 level tbs of clear honey

Method
Cream margarine, sugar, lemon rind and honey until light and fluffy. Beat in the eggs with a little flour. Fold in the remaining flour and put in the loaf tin and bake at 375°F or 180°C for 30 minutes. Heat together the lemon juice and honey till boiling and spoon over the cake. Leave in tin till cool.

HONEY SCOTTISH PANCAKES

120 gm (4 oz) Self Raising Flour
Pinch of baking powder
30 gm (1 oz) margarine
1 rounded tbs of honey
1 egg
5 tbs milk

Method
Rub margarine into the flour. Make a well in the centre and add honey, egg and milk. Mix well.

Rub a butter paper over girdlle or heavy based frying pan. When hot drop dessertspoonfuls onto it. When bubbles appear, turn over and brown the other side. Remove to a cooling tray with a tea towel on it and cover.

GIRDLE SCONES

240 gm (8 oz) Self Raising Flour
Pinch of salt
30 gm (1 oz) butter
1 level dsp runny honey
1/4 pint milk

Method
Heat a girdle or heavy frying pan over a gentle heat. Rub butter into flour, add honey and milk mixing with a knife. Turn onto a floured board and knead very lightly, shaping it into a round 1/2 inch thick. Cut into quarters , cook gently for about 7 minutes on each side or until cooked through.

BORDER TART

Rich pastry
60 gm (2 oz) Self Raising Flour
420 gm (14 oz) plain flour
120 gm (5 oz) caster sugar
300 gm (10 oz) margarine
1 egg

Method for pastry
Rub margarine into flour and sugar. Add egg and knead well. Unrequired pastry may be kept for up to two weeks in the fridge.

Line a sponge tin with pastry. Do not cook.

Filling
30 gm (1 oz) margarine
30 gm (1 oz) honey
60 gm (2 oz) soft brown sugar
1 cup of mixed dried fruit, preferably including some dates.
1 egg

Method
Mix all together and pour into pastry case. Bake in a moderate oven, 325°F or 160°C, till lightly browned.

BLACK BUN

10 inch cake tin

Pastry
360 gm (12 oz) of plain flour
Pinch of salt
120 gm (4 oz) margarine
Water

Method
Rub the margarine into the flour. Add enough water to make a firm dough. Line the tin with thinly rolled pastry, cutting a circle for top and bottom and a strip for sides. Seal well at the bottom edge.

Mixture
480 gm (1 lb) Self Raising Flour
960 gm (2 lb) raisins
960 gm (2 lb) currants
1/4 tsp black pepper
1 level tsp cinnamon
1 tbs whisky
120 gm (4 oz) honey
120 gm (4 oz) brown sugar
1 level tsp ground ginger
1/2 pint milk

Method
Mix all the dry ingredients and add milk to moisten. Turn mixture into tin lined with pastry. Put pastry lid on sealing well. Make 4 holes with a skewer right through. Prick pastry and brush with egg. Bake in a moderate oven 350°F or 180°C for 1 hour and 300°F or 150°C for two hours. Cool in the tin.

DUNDEE CAKE

8" cake tin lined

240 gm (8 oz) margarine or butter
120 gm (4 oz) caster sugar
120 gm (4 oz) honey
5 eggs
330 gm (11 oz) plain flour
1/2 tsp baking powder
720 gm (1 1/2 lb) mixed fruit
120 gm (4 oz) each cherries and peel
60 gm (2 oz) ground almonds
Whole almonds to decorate, blanched

Method
Warm the oven. Cream butter, sugar and honey. Add the egg and flour alternatively. Add dried fruit and ground almonds. Mix well. Pour into cake tin spreading evenly across. Decorate with whole almonds. Bake at 250°F or 130°C for 3 1/2 hours

SELKIRK BANNOCK

Dough
240 gm (1/2 lb) strong white flour
30 gm (1 oz) butter
30 gm (1 oz) soft margarine
30 gm (1 oz) honey
1 switched egg, saving some for brushing the top
1/4 pint water
Pinch of salt
1 tsp quick dried yeast

Method
Mix all together and knead for 10 minutes.

Work in 480 gm (1 lb) sultanas, shape into two circles, about 7" diameter, and leave to rise in a warm place till doubled. Heat oven to 325°F or 160°C. Brush the top with beaten egg and bake for 1/2 hour.

If using a bread machine you may want to use double the amount of dough in which case half can be made into a fruit loaf using some sultanas and chopped walnuts.

PUGGIES

Makes 12 – 14

Paste for outside
240 gm (8 oz) plain flour
120 gm (4 oz) margarine
60 gm (2 oz) caster sugar
1/4 pint water

Method
Mix flour and sugar. Rub in the margarine. Blend in water using a knife for mixing. Don't make too moist.
Roll the pastry out thinly and cut out circles about 5" (I use a pot lid as a cutter).

Filling
240gm (8oz) strong flour
1 level tsp baking soda
1 rounded tsp spice
120 gm (4 oz) runny honey
30 gm (1 oz) margarine
30 gm (1 oz) caster sugar
90 gm (3 oz) milk, approx.

Method
Mix dried ingredients and rub in the margarine. Put the honey in a well in the centre, add the milk mixing a little at a time to make a soft dough.

Cut the filling into 12 – 14 pieces. Roll into a ball and place in the middle of the dough, flattening slightly. Wet the edges of the dough and gather together covering the filling. Turn over and roll out to about 3 inches. With a sharp knife make two parallel slits through the top layer of the pastry. Place on a greased baking sheet and bake at 400°F or 190°C for about 15 minutes.

GOOSEBERRY CAKE

3 x 1 lb loaf tins, lined

480 gm (1 lb) green gooseberries

Crumble topping
120gm (4 oz) Self Raising Flour
90 gm (3 oz) caster sugar
90 gm (3 oz) butter
1 tbs water

Cake base
180 gm (6 oz) Self Raising Flour
Pinch of salt
120 gm (4 oz) butter
1 tbs runny honey

60 gm (2 oz) caster sugar
2 eggs
½ tsp vanilla essence
Milk to mix

Method
Make the cake mixture by creaming all together and spread over the base of the tins. Layer the gooseberries over the cake. Mix the crumble, flour, sugar and butter all together, add the water till lumpy and spread over the gooseberries. Sprinkle over a little icing sugar and bake for 1 hour 350°F or 180°C. Cool in the tin.

CARROT AND ORANGE LOAF WITH HONEY

Preheat oven to 350°F or 180°C. Lightly grease and base line a 2 lb loaf tin.

1 orange
150 gm (5 oz) soft margarine
150 gm (5 oz) light Muscavado sugar
180 gm (6 oz) carrots, peeled and grated
2 eggs beaten
210 gm (7 oz) Self Raising Flour
1 tsp baking powder
½ tsp mixed spice
1 tbs milk

To finish – 2 tbs clear honey

Method
Finely grate the orange rind. Cut away the pith and slice the orange thinly. Place rind in a large bowl and add the margarine, sugar, carrot, eggs, flour, baking powder and spice. Mix well until thoroughly blended. Add the milk, if necessary, to give a dropping consistency. Spoon into prepared tin. Bake the cake in a preheated oven for 1 hour or until just firm to the touch. Remove the cake from the oven and arrange slices of orange over the top. Brush with the honey and return to the oven and bake for a further 15 minutes or until a skewer placed into the centre of the cake comes out clean. Leave to cool in the tin for a few minutes then turn out and leave to cool completely on a wire rack.

Index of Recipes